APOLOGY
The Gift We Give
Our Young Adults

PARENT

Apology

Forgive-ness

Letting Go

Saying No

Identity

Under-standing

Love

Forgive-ness

Under-standing

Love

Independence

YOUNG ADULT

Jack Stoltzfus, PhD

Apology: The Gift We Give Our Young Adults

This is a third in a series of books on parental practices that help support the young adult's task of independence.

Can You Speak Millennial "ese"? How to Understand and Communicate with Your Young Adult
Love to Let Go: Loving Our Kids into Adulthood
Apology: The Gift We Give Our Young Adults
Forgiveness: The Gift We Share with Our Young Adults and Ourselves
Supportive Integrity: Parenting Our Young Adults with Love and Backbone
Growing Apart: Letting Go of Our Young Adults

ISBN 978-0-9994563-6-1

Dr. Jack Stoltzfus
www.parentslettinggo.com

Contents

Preface

This book is the third in a series of six that describe the crucial practices parents need to strengthen in order to facilitate the launching of their young adult. Like the others in the series, it was written to address the need for a specific "letting-go practice" and offer practical actions a parent can take. The development of these practices grew out of the author's experience as a psychologist working with parents who were troubled and confused about how to help their young adult move toward mature independence. This is for and about the parents of young adults.

This book and others don't contain the magic answers to what a parent can do to change, fix, or persuade a young adult to take a specific course of action in their lives. It does give parents guidance on how to communicate, engage, support, and let go in ways that help parents feel less worried, anxious, guilty, and frustrated. If you find yourself constantly reaching out to your young adult, worrying about them during the day, or lying awake at night wondering if they will make it, then these books are for you.

In *Apology: The Gift We Give Our Young Adults*, you will find guidance in how to deal with issues of the past that keep you bound emotionally to your young adult in unhealthy ways. One parent said to me: "Being a parent is one big guilt trip." This book is about how to let go of feelings such as guilt, sadness, resentment, and regret, and thoughts such as being a failure or things we should have done. Such feelings and thoughts keep us bound to our young adults in unhealthy ways and can lead to actions that interfere with the launching process.

There are several books written on the importance of apology, which are referenced in the last chapter, however, they can be somewhat daunting to read and apply. This book is written to be a practical guide about parental apology that can help you identify the need for apology and impact of apology as well as how to go about it. In the Parents Letting Go workshops I have done, I have found most parents want concise, practical—what to do—information on these practices. My hope is that you find this book to be just that, and more importantly you take the messages to heart and apply the concepts. My belief is that you can read this book in an evening and make a decision on an action to take that will make a difference in you, your young adult, and your relationship with them.

About the Author

Dr. Jack Stoltzfus is a licensed psychol-ogist practicing in Shoreview, Minnesota. He received his PhD in counseling psychology from the University of Wisconsin-Madison. The focus of his PhD dissertation was on defining and measuring healthy adolescent separation from parents. His private practice is focused on parents and young adults. Dr. Stoltzfus has worked with parents and their young adult children within the context of a chemical dependency day treatment program, inpatient mental health facilities, a child guidance clinic, a youth service agency, and a private practice for more than thirty years. He has three grown and married young adult children who represent the millennial and early Gen X generations.

CHAPTER 1

Why Wait to Apologize?

A woman, now a mother herself, leaned closer to hear what her dying father wanted to say to her. She had been steadfastly caring for him during his lengthy battle with cancer. Inside she wondered why she was so diligently tending to him, since this man, humbled by cancer, had been a terrible, abusive, and raging alcoholic father. She grew up in a home where the only thing that was predictable was his unpredictability. With such a parent she never knew when the next drunken attack would come. As she leaned in, this father with tears in his eyes told her how sorry he was for the way he had treated her and asked for her forgiveness.

My guess is this deathbed confession and request for forgiveness is a scene that happens way too often. All those who hear words like these in the final hours want to think they are sincere and not just preparation for the day of judgment. But such apologies, sincere or otherwise, have to be bittersweet. They beg the question: Why were these words not said many years ago when the sincerity could have been demonstrated by changes of behavior?

Many who have had abusive, neglectful, or in other ways inattentive parents who did not live up to their responsibilities of loving, supporting, and protecting their children would like to hear an acknowledgment of these shortcomings and an apology. Can we live without this? Sure, many of us do. But to hear an apology is a way of the parent saying: "It was not you, it was me." Since children have inherited imperfect parents, the likelihood of mistakes being made is inevitable. And we don't know the extent to which these mistakes may still leave wounds with our children.

Why would we wait to apologize?

CHAPTER 2

Apology: One of Six Practices

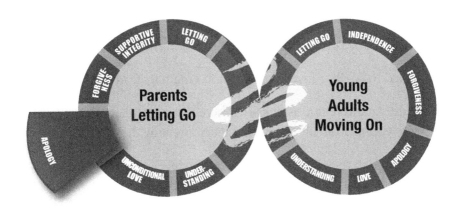

Apology is one of the six practices parents can use to successfully launch their young adult. In my conversations with parents, some were not familiar with the terms "launch" or "failure to launch." Launch refers to the process in which parents and young adults collaborate in the transition of the young adult into mature adulthood. When the young adult has achieved this, they can be described as autonomous and positively connected to their parents. Failure to launch is characterized by lack of autonomy and/or strained relationships with the parents. It is not just about living at home or living away from home, but achieving emotional independence as well as financial independence. In earlier books I have described the practices of *understanding* and *unconditional love*. In this book, the practice of *parental apology* is described as a necessary process of letting go of past actions that keep the parent and young adult emotionally bound.

Basic Assumptions of Letting Go

There are basic assumptions or beliefs that underlie the process of supportive emancipation or letting go in love. As parents we:

- Cannot control our young adults.

- Are not responsible for their decisions or actions.

- Are responsible for our decisions and actions.

- Will not use the past to excuse our actions or theirs.

- Need to balance love (support) and emancipation (letting go).

- Understand relationships are inherently reciprocal—how we treat our young adult children will determine how they treat us.

- Change starts with us—thinking, behaving, and feeling differently.

The practice of apology is based largely upon two assumptions. First is our responsibility for our actions and decisions, specifically those that have hurt the relationship with our young adults. Second is the need to change first. In presenting all of these practices, I have made the argument that parents need to take the lead, be the change they want in the relationship, and show the way. In the end, will apologizing make a difference in the relationship? Yes, in as much as it will free us as parents from feelings and thoughts that keep us painfully bound to our young adults and open new space in our hearts to feel differently. Review the first assumption: we cannot control our young adults. Apology will also free young adults from feelings of anger, resentment, and blame that may be keeping them stuck in both the relationship with us and in life. We give them a chance to let go of the past as we do the same.

Will the young adult change if we apologize? We won't know, but not knowing can't be an excuse for not doing.

We know the power of apology to heal relationships but we don't always practice it. When our children were young we were quick to tell them to apologize to a sibling or friend when they had hit that person or grabbed a toy that did not belong to them. Although unclear as to the understanding of this imposed ritual, children learned something about the need to say "sorry" when they hurt another. Unfortunately, we as parents were not always as quick to say we were sorry to the child or spouse and model this value and process. Neglecting or resisting the practice of apologizing can avoid dealing with underlying feelings and thoughts that signal an apology may be needed. The next chapter begins with a brief quiz that can help you identify any underlying feelings that point to the value of apologizing.

CHAPTER 3

Feelings and Thoughts Quizzes

Take the Feelings Quiz

Feelings are often the barometer of a relationship and can signal a need to apologize. Check any of the feelings below that you have had regarding your relationship with your young adult (either now or in the past).

_____Guilt	_____Being stuck
_____Shame	_____Ambivalence
_____Sadness	_____Criticism
_____Regret	_____Responsibility
_____Resentment	_____Grief
_____Remorse	_____Loss
_____Failure	_____Sorrow
_____Inadequacy	_____Alienation
_____Frustration	_____Depression
_____Bitterness	_____Despair
_____Self-blame	_____Disappointment
_____Embarrassment	

There are multiple reasons for these feelings, and not all of them signal a need for apology. Most parents who attend my workshops or those I see in my private practice are experiencing one or more of these feelings. You can also address the need for an apology to your young adults by looking at your *thoughts*—what they say about your young adult or yourself.

Take the Thoughts Quiz

Some thoughts may indicate an apology is needed. Check any of the statements below that might apply to the history of your relationship to your young adult. Think of these statements related to each child separately.

_____1. I have regrets about my parenting.

_____2. I know I said or did things that were wrong.

_____3. I think my parenting may have contributed to problems my children have today.

_____4. I wish I could have a "do over" for some situation or time in the past.

_____5. My young adult believes I did or didn't do something in the past that has led to hurt and anger toward me.

_____6. I believe that I expected too much or too little of my child.

_____7. I did something unintentional that has caused distance and hurt between my child and me.

_____8. I failed to protect or intervene in a situation with my child that has led to distance and hurt between my child and me.

_____ 9. I got divorced.

_____10. I didn't give my young adult enough time or attention when they were growing up. I was too busy.

_____11. I wasn't affectionate enough.

_____12. I was inconsistent in my parenting.

_____13. I was overly critical.

_____14. I yelled, hit, or spanked out of anger.

_____15. I was depressed or anxious and couldn't be there emotionally for my child.

_____16. I drank alcohol in my early pregnancy before I knew I was pregnant and think that damaged my child.

My guess is that I have been able to get your attention with the two quizzes above since it's hard to believe that any of us don't check one or more of these items. That's actually the positive news about taking such a survey—we all fall short of perfect parenthood. You may feel angry toward me for calling attention to our shortcomings, but please be assured that I am not trying to add to the guilt you may already feel. Adults who have parented are the most guilt-ridden segment of our society. And that's a big segment. So don't think you are in any way alone if you checked one or more items above. I don't want to compound this feeling but to help relieve it.

At this stage, my intent is to help you identify the potential need to move forward with an apology to your child. There is a saying that goes: You have to feel it to heal it.

Recognition of a need to apologize by becoming aware of our feelings and thoughts is a first step toward healing and letting go.

At the end of the day, it's your choice whether you believe there is a reason or need to apologize or whether you think it would serve a purpose. In some cases you may have apologized to the point that your young adult has said "enough." My ninety-six-year-old mother who lives in Florida tends to lapse into apologies when I visit her, and I have had to reassure that she was a good mother and I carry no malice toward her. So if you are all apologized out, can you learn anything from this book? I think so and encourage you to read on.

CHAPTER 4

What Constitutes an Apology?

Let's start with a definition.

Apology: A statement of remorse, regret, and responsibility for:
• Having done or said something wrong.
• Not being able to do or be something.
• Having offended another intentionally or unintentionally.

An apology is sincere and respectful, and demonstrates under-standing—if not empathy—for the recipient. Apologies need to originate and emanate from the heart. We give apologies because we care about the young adult and feel it is the right thing to. It has to be heartfelt.

Take a closer look at the elements of an apology. First, it is a statement of remorse based upon a heartfelt understanding of the impact of your actions on another. This typically involves some level of empathy or compassion. However, not being able to identify or empathize with the emotional impact of an action on another is not an excuse for not apologizing.

Second, it is a statement of regret—"I'm sorry"—because you believe your actions had a hurtful impact on another. With both the expressions of remorse and regret, it is important to be sincere and contrite when expressing regret or it will not be well received. Your tone and body language need to match your words.

Third, and most importantly, it requires one to take responsibility for the communication, decision, or action that was hurtful. In Lewicki's research on apology, the most important element is the willingness of the offender to take responsibility for their actions.[1] It starts with identifying what we have done that requires an apology regardless of what the other person did or said. We take responsibility for our part no matter what.

You have to be willing to say, it's my fault, but you don't have to say, it's all my fault.

Fourth, acknowledging you can't change the past but making a determined commitment to change your behavior that was offensive going forward is one of the best if not the only way to demonstrate your sincerity.

Changing one's behavior is the sign of a true apology.

Two additional elements could be considered by the person making an apology, but may depend on the situation.

Make an offer to make amends or to try to correct the situation. This may not always be possible with actions that have happened in the past that can't be undone. However, the expression of a sincere desire to make up for what one has done reinforces your desire to restore the relationship. At a minimum one's most important amend is to not repeat the offense. Asking the young adult what you can do to make amends is the best approach. Perhaps there was some favoritism shown to one sibling over another and something could be done to address this.

A request for forgiveness. Although this can be done in many cases of past actions by parents, it's critical that the parent gives the young adult space and time to consider this and ultimately decide not to offer it. As such, the parent can't offer an apology with the expectation or hope of forgiveness because this can be perceived as contrived. If you don't receive an expression of forgiveness and are upset, hurt, or resentful, you should reconsider your motives for apologizing. The main work you need to do as parent is to apologize for past grievances. If you receive forgiveness, that's a bit of icing on the cake. Incidentally, Lewicki, whose research was with college students and adults and not focused on parental apology, found the request for forgiveness the least important element in an apology.

The hard work for us parents is to say we are sorry without any expectations.

Why Is Apologizing Hard?

Parents may think that to admit to mistakes erodes the image they try to preserve of being competent and right. They also may think those admissions could undermine the child's confidence in and compliance with parents' future expectations. To some extent when children are younger and of school age, they may idolize their parents and believe they can do no wrong. However, there comes a point when the child begins to

see the flaws and shortcomings of the parent. This can be upsetting to the child to realize that the parent can make mistakes, fail to meet promises, and do things that seem to contradict the parent's messages or values. Most children adapt at this point, but if a parent continues to act as if whatever they say or do is always correct, a distance can grow and between the parent and the child. This can lead to the child questioning other parental statement or actions and ultimately a loss of the credibility the parent is trying to maintain. Men tend to have greater difficulty apologizing than women.[2]

My father never apologized to me in my growing up years, or if he did I do not remember . . . and think I would have. As I observed my father's relationship with his father, I was aware that his father had a need to be right and most likely never apologized to my father. This was an "old school" type of thinking—that if I apologized I would lose my credibility or my control. In fact the lack of apology in the face of clear actions deserving an apology lead to a compliance and credibility problem for children.

   My relationship with my father was emotionally distant for many of my years from fairly early childhood until my midtwenties. I would have appreciated it if he would have taken the lead and acknowledged this distance and both apologized and made efforts to close the gap. Because of this distance and a sense that my father was not willing to be vulnerable and open with me, my relating to him became contentious and our relationship suffered. My reactivity to him was both out of hurt about the distance but also a need to connect emotionally. I found a way to engage emotionally with my father by reacting angrily to things he said.

   Not unlike me, many young adults will engage through negative emotional reactivity if they can't find positive avenues. Fortunately, as I describe in my book Love to Let Go, *my journey with my father ended well, and I feel no anger or hurt for an apology I never received. That said, it sure would have been nice to have had an apology and a closer relationship with my dad that an apology would have fostered. Don't wait.*

   Parents may feel that to admit to mistakes and apologize is to acknowledge they have failed as a parent. This is unfortunate for two reasons. First, it's important to distinguish between mistakes or failures and *being* a failure. The former constitutes guilt and the latter constitutes shame. Shame reflects a belief that as a parent you are a failure, a mistake, or fundamentally flawed. At some of our worst times we may feel so bad that we wish we had not been a parent. This is confusing a mistake with *being* a mistake. Don't go there; it's a dark place resulting from irrational thinking. None of us are mistakes.

   Guilt, on the other hand, can be useful and constructive in identifying mistakes we made and ways we could have made better decisions. These mistakes and poor decisions comprise our basic, imperfect humanity and are an appropriate basis for apology. Far from being a sign of failure, apologies allow for the opening up of a channel for intimacy. Brené Brown eloquently argues for vulnerability as the route to intimacy.[3]

Like Brown, I have always found that sharing my shortcomings and failures leads to deeper relational connections than sharing my strengths or accomplishments.

Apologies are viewed as a sign of weakness. This view is particularly strong in the world of politics and business. Such admissions of mistakes have risks. When I was leading a health promotion initiative at a local company in the late nineties, I made a mistake in not screening certain materials sent out that contained numerous mistakes. I asked to appear before the human resources operating committee to acknowledge my mistake and apologize. I felt emotionally naked in front of the committee, but my apology was well received. My guess is, however, it didn't add to my leadership brand as a strong leader. At no time in my twenty-six year career at that company did I see anyone make such a public apology. If I had to do it over again, would I do the same thing? You bet. Sometimes you just have to do what you know is right. As a parent, acknowledging your mistakes is the right thing to do.

Resistance to apology may arise out of pride and a belief that the other person was to blame as well. Apologizing for one's part of a mistake in a situation does not excuse the behavior of the other. It's just saying: "I'm taking responsibility for my part in what went wrong." To resist acknowledging one's failures because of a belief the other person did something wrong or the child caused the parent to react a certain way will either cause one to resist apologizing or lead to an "I'm sorry but . . ." non-apology.

Value relationships over pride.

Parents may believe that to apologize invites other accusations by their young adult or could be used against them at a future date. It's possible the apology may be used to excuse current behavior that the young adult does not want to change. Or your young adult may take the opportunity to dredge up other past actions deserving of an apology. Yes, this risk exists, but surfacing other things of the past that bothers your young adult is a good thing that can lead to freeing both parties.

If the apology relates to some ongoing behavior that the parent acknowledges and indicates a desire to change, then the parent must take responsibility for ensuring that the behavior changes. And your young adult can rightly call you out for this. If the parent slips back into the old behavior, the parent needs to say again they are sorry and promise to do better. Obviously, a parent can't maintain credibility if they constantly say they are sorry and repeat the same inappropriate behavior.

Once when I was coaching an executive at a local company on changing some bad behavior, he found himself falling back into old patterns and had to go back on several occasions to his direct report and apologize. My colleague who observed this leader's behavior and his apologies said: "We will know he has truly changed when he no longer has to apologize."

Sustainable change is the proof of an apology.

Parents may fear the reaction to apologizing and bringing up an offense in the past. They may claim that it's best to leave sleeping dogs lie, but this can reflect an underlying fear of facing the truth. My clinical experience has proven that in most cases the "truth" does set one free.

Parents who lack an experience of apology from their parent may find apologizing to their own child difficult. Sometimes there is a conscious or subconscious resistance characterized by a belief that I never got an apology so why should my adult child receive one. Why not push through this resistance and break the generational pattern that you know hurt you?

Don't fail to reach out to your kids just because your parents didn't do this for you. Be the one who changes this generational pattern.

CHAPTER 6

Why Apologize?

The benefits of apologizing to your young adult for both the young adult and parent are many. Check the top five reasons you would consider apologizing to your young adult.

_____ 1. You acknowledge that you have fallen short in some way as a parent. Incidentally, you aren't divulging some secret to your young adult.

_____ 2. You model humility and vulnerability as an imperfect human being and invite this from your child.

_____ 3. You recognize and accept your responsibility for an act and not leave doubt that the child was somehow failed. It sets the young adult free.

_____ 4. You restore a belief in an important value by accepting responsibility for failing to demonstrate that value. For example, if you have always told your children to be honest and fail on some occasion to do this, your apology is a way of saying you made a mistake but that you continue to value honesty.

_____ 5. A sincere apology sends a message you care about your young adult and your relationship, and you want to restore the trust that was lost.

_____ 6. Although a parent's apology is fundamentally a gift to the child, it is also a gift to the parent as it allows the parent to let go of feelings and thoughts that have bound them to the child negatively.

_____ 7. It models understanding of the importance of saying "I'm sorry" and empathy in connecting to the hurt the young adult has or may have felt as a result of some offense on the part of the parent.

_____ 8. Apologies allow parents to share their imperfections and identify with their young adult as they struggle with their own imperfections. It's a source of identification and solidarity.

_____ 9. It's a teaching opportunity for you and a learning opportunity for your child around values of honesty, making mistakes, taking responsibility, apologizing, and making amends.

_____10. Confession of mistakes and apologizing enable parents to be healthier and better people. All major religions encourage the confession of transgressions. The AA community has a saying that applies: "You are only as sick as your secrets." Shame is often the glue that keeps people stuck in the past.

_____11. Apology is the first step toward restoration and reconciliation in the parent/young adult relationship.

_____12. Although forgiveness is not a given when one apologizes, the lack of apology almost always assures that forgiveness won't happen.

Although there are many benefits to parental apology for both young adults and parents, how does this practice help to launch young adults into mature independence?

CHAPTER 7

Apologize to Free Your Young Adult

Reasons for apologizing were identified in the feelings and thoughts quizzes in chapter 3. So how does the role of apologizing help launch your young adult? The healthy state of separation between a young adult and the young adult's parent is characterized by connected autonomy. This is a state in

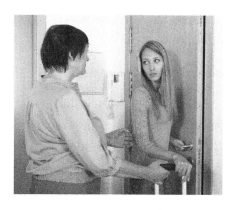

which the young adult feels free to be themselves, whether this aligns with the parent's expectations or not, and simultaneously maintains a loving connection to the parent.

Healthy separation

There are a variety of reasons why young adults fail to transition into mature adulthood and mature relationships with their parents. Many factors contribute to the struggles young adults have with the development tasks of identity, independence, and intimacy. These include external factors such as the influence of friends and the economic environment. Temperament and other personality factors can explain some differences between young adult members in the same family. Complications of physical, mental, and learning disabilities play an important confounding role. Finally, the history and current relationship with parents contribute to some degree to the success or failure of the launch process. Although parents can't change the past, they can acknowledge the past and the impact it had on the young adult. Acknowledging and apologizing for past mistakes or shortcomings have great potential to overcome impediments to mature adulthood.

Negative Enmeshment

Young adults who harbor resentment toward their parents as a result of perceptions they have regarding the parents' treatment of them, keep them bound in a state of negative enmeshment. The word *enmeshment* may sound like psychobabble, but it means being stuck, entangled, and ensnared. Both parents and young adults can exhibit enmeshment behavior that becomes hard to resist by the other party. It's not just a young adult problem. The practices in this book are aimed at helping parents avoid enmeshment and move to the healthy state of loving separation.

Negative enmeshment exhibited by a young adult is characterized by attacks on the parents, blaming, accusations, excusing of behavior, and explaining current failures in their own life on current or past actions of their parents. This internal mindset will affect their relationships with friends, potential partners, and bosses as well as how they approach life's responsibilities. One young adult I saw in my practice said, "My mother never loved me as much as my siblings, never gave me the attention I needed." Such indictments relegate the young adult to a life of victimhood and failing because they harbor a built-in excuse for not succeeding. The following diagram shows this state of enmeshment where the connections between the young adult and parent are negatively charged. My relationship with my father in my young adult years was characterized this way.

Negatively enmeshed

Growing into maturity for this negatively enmeshed young adult means believing they are no longer inevitably programmed to struggle and fail due to the parents' actions. So what can parents do? What purpose can an apology serve in this case? Although not automatic, a sincere apology from the parents reduces the basis for continuing to be angry and resentful. Saying, "I'm sorry and I wish I could do some things over again, but I'm willing to work on changing going forward," has the power to diffuse the anger and hurt that sustains the negative enmeshment. But it doesn't just help the young adult; it helps you as a parent.

The impact on you as a parent is to free you up from the negative emotions that have bound you in unhealthy ways to these young adults. When you apologize, you release the guilt, the regret, the sadness, and the self-blame, and you can move forward without these emotions controlling your actions. If you continue to feel guilty and sad about your past, you overreact in defensive or self-pitying ways fueled by these emotions. The net result of both parties harboring these types of negative emotions is that the relationship suffers. Since relationships are highly reciprocal, personal attacks, defensiveness, blaming, anger, and being cut-off are the common denominators.

Positive Enmeshment

Some young adults and parents may be caught in a state of positive enmeshment. In this state the young adult does not feel free to contradict or challenge the parent. They do not believe they can be themselves without risking the closeness they feel with them. In this situation, they have a hard time making decisions on their own and constantly look for approval from the parents. Parents are positively enmeshed in supporting, if not controlling, their young adult and hold on too tightly because of anxiety or fear—maybe they can't make it on their own. Parents also may hang on too tightly because they fear the loss of closeness to their child. By doing so the parent binds the child emotionally and behaviorally to them and forestalls the launch process. When this occurs the apology of the parent may need to be more in terms of over involvement, over control, and over dependence on the young adult's connection.

Positively enmeshed

Apology Is Dynamic

These different characterizations of the relationship between the parent and the young adult are not static. The two types of enmeshment situations and the accompanying opportunities for apology can change and often are more dynamic than the model indicates. Often the dynamic is best understood as a dance between the parents and the young adult. At one time the parent may lean in to provide support and encouragement to the young adult only to experience rejection as the young adult pushes back and distances themself. On another occasion the parent may step back to give more space and let go only to find the young adult moving closer and complaining about lack of caring and support.

Much frustration for both parties can be described in terms of this push-pull dynamic. I have often used the metaphor of two people dancing but to different music. It can feel very strange and confusing for both parties. The parents may be required to undertake a more real time use of apology when they inadvertently step on the young adult's toes or lean back and miss the reach of the young adult when connection is most needed. There is no set choreography to this supporting and letting-go process. But apologizing with the right heart and in the right way can heal a lot of sore toes and bruises.

CHAPTER 8

What to Avoid in an Apology

Saying, I'm sorry "but" or "if" or "however." This is a contradictory apology because these words essentially negate the words "I'm sorry" and suggest that the person isn't really sorry. Once my wife and I began to practice avoiding these words, the number of arguments that started up again after the sorry statement de-

creased dramatically. It was hard for me to implement this practice. I was used to defending myself routinely as a child and finding someone else or something else to blame. To just say "I'm sorry" and take responsibility for my part in the problem without any qualifiers left me somewhat frustrated. Be aware of the "buts."

Sorry . . . but you had a part in this

Sorry . . . but we all make mistakes

Sorry . . . but you're not perfect

Sorry . . . but it was an accident

Sorry . . . but I was just trying to be helpful

Sorry . . . but you shouldn't take it so personally

Sorry . . . but (other)

Also avoid the "if" statements that are non-apologies, such as, "I'm sorry if you didn't understand, if you felt I was condescending, if you were offended."

Blanket apologies are less effective than those that specify what the parent has done. Blanket apologies such as, "I'm sorry I was such a bad parent" or "I'm sorry for everything I ever did wrong as a parent" will come off insincere at best. In fact it is better to identify your specific contribution to a difficult time and take responsibility for that piece. Taking responsibility for a pattern in how you treated the young adult is also appropriate. For instance, "I'm sorry I was so critical of you and led you to believe you could never satisfy me."

Saying, I'm sorry you feel . . . or I made you feel . . . or that you took this wrong . . . or that you misunderstood me. These are not real apologies but rather blame the other person and are underhanded apologies. Another example of an underhanded apology is to say something sarcastic, and when the receiver of this message indicates they were offended, you say I'm sorry I was joking. This type of "sorry" is very difficult to process because it is clear the person meant the offensive comment but then turns it back on you as if they didn't mean it and you didn't get their humor. Even if you said or did something in jest, if your young adult experienced it as painful, apologize. Don't try to explain it away or turn it back on the young adult.

Saying, I would say I am sorry but I didn't mean to say or do something is not an apology. It's an excuse. The intention is not the critical factor. The action and the perception of the receiver are the critical basis for an apology. We routinely apologize if we bump someone in line at the grocery store or inadvertently step on someone's foot, even though these were not intentional acts. So the lack of intention is not an excuse to not apologize.

Giving a partial apology for example, if someone swore at you and then slapped you, but only apologized for swearing. This leaves the victim feeling that you really aren't taking full responsibility for your actions. According to research from *The Journal of Personality and Social Psychology* reported in *Psychology Today*, such partial apologizers feel worse than full apologizers. The partial apologizers introduce a new type of dishonesty by trying to avoid or cover up the full extent of their offense.[4]

Saying, "I did the best I could as a parent." This is a veiled apology that essentially absolves the parent of responsibility for the treatment of the child in growing up. After all, if the parent did the best they could then how could they be responsible for problems that occurred? The implication is that something else went wrong and the parent is not responsible because they did the best they could.

When I host my Parents Letting Go workshops, I offer an opportunity for any perfect parents who are in the audience to excuse themselves. So far I have not had anyone get up and walk out. We have to own up to our failure as parents to always do what was right. What parent can't look back and say I should have . . . I wish I hadn't . . . if I could do it over I would . . . Much better to admit that we made mistakes and to own up to them and apologize for those that have damaged the relationship with our children.

Saying you're sorry to the wrong person. For instance telling a spouse you are sorry for something you did to your child but not telling the child. Worse yet is asking the spouse to apologize on your behalf.

Saying you're sorry without any change in behavior. Sometimes this type of sorry is just an excuse for continuing to do something that's offensive or can be perceived as insincere if the person keeps up the offensive behavior. Saying I'm sorry doesn't give one a free pass for repeating offensive behavior.

Saying I'm sorry repeatedly to the point that it is ineffective or annoying. For various reasons, some individuals have come to believe they are responsible for anything that goes wrong. As such they are quick to apologize for almost anything even when they didn't do anything wrong. They fear offending another person and quickly apologize. There's almost a sense that they are apologizing for being alive. Use apologies sparingly and targeted to a specific offense.

CHAPTER 9

When Should You Apologize?

Many of the reasons for apologizing can be found in the thoughts quiz you completed earlier, but here are a few more reasons specific to the young adult stage. Which of these thoughts indicate a need for you to apologize? Can you think of other reasons?

_____ 1. I realized I made a mistake or failed to live up to the standard I established for myself as a parent.

_____ 2. When my young adult brings up a decision, communication, or action they experienced in growing up that was hurtful.

_____ 3. When I have been dishonest.

_____ 4. When I failed to keep a promise.

_____ 5. When I was observed in a behavior that was inconsistent with the values I have espoused.

_____ 6. For not holding them accountable for their behavior.

_____ 7. For overindulging them and contributing to an entitlement mindset.

_____ 8. For not telling them how much I loved them.

_____ 9. For not encouraging them in some special area of interest they had.

_____10. When your young adult attributes or uses your actions of the past to excuse their current behavior.

CHAPTER 10

Ask Your Young Adult

Are you brave enough and secure enough to ask your young adult what apologies they would like to hear from you? Sometimes what we think should be a basis for an apology is not the same as what they may have in  mind. This doesn't mean that we should not still apologize for something we regret. We can do both.

Following are some questions that can lead you into a dialogue with your young adult and enable you to acknowledge and address any unresolved feelings and perceptions they may have about your parenting. But first, here are some suggestions and reminders before you approach your young adult with the questions.

Suggestions for Meeting with Your Young Adult

Invite them to meet with you outside their home or yours to answer some questions relative to your parenting of them over the years. If they balk at a meeting, ask them if they would answer the questions through text or other electronic media. Tweeting may not be the best vehicle. While face-to-face is the optimal venue for this type of communication, getting their perceptions and input is more important.

Listen nonjudgmentally. This is discussed in depth in the first practice book on the topic of understanding your young adult. It means listening for understanding and clarification. Check out what you have heard them say both at the level of content and feelings. To be real clear, here's an example.

- Young adult shares: "You took my older brother to a baseball game and left me home because you said I was too young. You never did take me to a game when I got older and I have never forgotten it."

- Father checks out what he heard: "So you were **hurt** and **disappointed** that *I took your older brother and not you to the ball game because I said you were too young.* And then you never did get to go with me when you were older." (This summarization captures the content and the feelings of hurt and disappointment.)

Note: The words in bold convey the father has heard the son's feelings. The words in italic convey he has heard why his son feels that way.

Tell them you will listen and take some notes, and then you want to meet again and respond to what they shared. Take some time to reflect on what your young adult has said and avoid defensiveness or explanations, such as, "Well, you see the reason I didn't . . ." A reminder: unintentional acts are appropriate reasons to apologize.

A colleague of mine, Sarah Bridges, suggests reflecting on what offenses your young adult brought to your attention and asking what might be two or three reasons this young adult would have been hurt by your actions. This is a good way to discover empathy with them and their experience.

Interview Questions to Surface Opportunities for a Parental Apology

1. What things would you like for me to have said as you were growing up?

2. What things, sayings, or other communications would you have wished I hadn't said?

3. What one or more things do you most remember about your experience with me that were disappointing? Follow-up question: Can you tell me how or why these were disappointing to you?

4. If we could go back to when you were a child, what one or two things would you like me to do differently?

5. What are some ways I could have been a better dad/mom to you when you were growing up?

6. What one or two things happened to you in our relationship that you still feel hurt or sad about?

7. What one or two things have I done or not done that have had a negative impact on your life today?

8. In the last two to three years, what have been the things I have done or said that have been most upsetting or frustrating to you?

9. What are some things I do or don't do today that are a source of frustration, hurt, or disappointment to you?

10. Is there anything that has happened in our relationship over the years for which you would like to hear me say, "I'm sorry?"

Once you have gathered this information, you can construct an apology following the protocol described in chapter 4. This can then be delivered to your young adult in person or in writing. My recommendation is to do both. First read the apology and then hand your son or daughter a copy. It could be a meaningful emotional connection to your young adult for you. And it may be for them as well, but again be careful you don't set yourself up for some type of response.

"Expectations are the root of all unhappiness."[5] Dennis Praeger

CHAPTER 11

Qualities Needed to Apologize

What qualities are needed to apologize to your young adult?

First, it takes a **willingness to be vulnerable**. Saying I'm sorry is humbling, particularly with our children to whom we have committed to being a good parent. You put yourself out there without any assurance of a receptive response.

Second, it requires a **commitment to be honest** and forthright in confessing what you have done that you regret. Our children at almost any age can detect if we are not being honest and sincere or fudging on our confession.

Third, **a recognition that we all make mistakes**, not to excuse our behavior but to recognize we are human. This belief humanizes us in the eyes of our young adults.

Fourth, it **takes love and compassion**. Love because we want to make right our relationship with the young adult; compassion because we understand and can empathize with their experience and want to reduce their pain.

Fifth, it takes a **willingness to be first**. We can't wait for them to offer us an apology for what they have done or for them to ask for an apology from us. We are the parents; we brought them into our lives, and we need to risk, take the high road, model, and be first.

Be brave . . . be vulnerable . . . be first.

Are You Ready to Craft Your Apology?

Review the following elements of an effective apology and consider them in your communication. If you draft a written apology, then go back and see if your communication contains these elements. (The sample letter of apology in the next chapter may give you additional ideas.)

- A heartfelt appreciation and remorse for the impact your actions had on your young adult, an experience of empathy and compassion.

- A sincere statement of regret—the "I'm sorry"—for the impact of your actions on your young adult whether intended or not.

- An expression of responsibility without any qualifiers, explanations, or excuses. You take responsibility for your part no matter what the other did or said.

- As able and appropriate: an offer to make amends or do what is needed to repair the damage to the relationship.

- As able and appropriate: a request for forgiveness while giving your young adult the freedom to say no without any repercussions.

CHAPTER 12

A Father's Apology to His Daughter

This heartfelt and sincere letter of apology from a father to his daughter includes the elements listed at the end of the previous chapter. As you read the letter, pay attention how it connects with you emotionally. Are there some ideas that you can use in your apology?

> *To my daughter,*
>
> *I wanted to take some time to reflect on my parenting of you as you were growing up and even now as you are thirty-eight years old. There are many fond memories of our relationship, particularly in the early years and especially when you were our first-born and only child. I was so proud of you and showed you off to all of my friends. You made funny faces and recited "Little Boy Blue" at this very early age. As the years went by and two other children arrived, our relationship changed and my initial time and attention to you was spread out over the other two. I'm sorry that I didn't do a good job of staying connected to you during this time. You were a happy, expressive, bright, young girl and deserved more of my attention. I was the one that dropped the ball on connecting to you, and I am sorry.*
>
> *When you hit your middle school years, you began to spend more time with friends and focused on things outside of the family.*

When you began to have trouble because of the challenge of taking both geometry and algebra in eighth grade, you began to doubt yourself even though we had affirmed your intelligence, as had all of your teachers to that point. Your experience had told you that you didn't have to study and could get straight A's. So when you began to falter in this eighth-grade course, you began to question your ability and resisted encouragement from me that you could and should be doing better. My mistake is that I didn't sit down with you and discuss the need to study and prepare, and that this was what was missing and not your ability. I think I always thought of you and told you that you were so smart and gave you the impression that academics should come easy for you. I realize now how saying that put undo pressure on you to perform, and when you struggled you doubted yourself. That doubt and loss of confidence is my fault and not yours. I should have picked up on this problem and been more engaged in helping you learn to prepare for school rather than communicate that you were so smart you could do school work by just showing up. I'm sorry.

Later on when you were worried about your mother and some health issues she was facing, I tended to think of you as capable enough to get through this on your own. I saw your anger at your mother and didn't pick up the extent to which this grew out of a fear you had about what was happening to her. Clearly the security you had felt in her strength and steadfastness was threatened. I look back and recognize now how upsetting and scary it was for you to see your mother struggling. Again, I failed to pick up on this and move closer to you and take you to breakfast, spend time with you, be reassuring, and more. I just wasn't there for you emotionally when you needed me and I am very, very sorry about this. It was my fault you did not have my attention and support at that time.

So I can't go back and have a do-over or I would do what was right and step up to meet your needs. If there are things I can do now or as we go forward as two adults to make up for these failures or be more sensitive and emotionally available to you, please let me know. I'm sure there are other things I did or did not do that you may still think about with some level of sadness or pain. Please know that I am open and receptive to hearing about these and won't blame you or defend myself. I will try to hear what I could have done differently and take full responsibility for my fail-

ure. So I have plenty more of "I'm sorry" available and want to be sure that I have owned and addressed all of these you need to hear.

So I love you dearly, have always loved you, and will always love you. If you can find it in your heart to forgive me for these things I didn't do for you as your dad I would appreciate this. That said, forgiveness is your choice and I don't have to have this, particularly if it's hard for you to do now or into the future. But know that your listening and acknowledging my communication to apologize for my failures as a father are enough.

Love, Dad

What If Your Young Adult Is Deceased?

The issue of apology is a particularly difficult challenge for a parent when they have lost a child. When there are things you believe you would have said or should have said and you didn't get a chance, the grieving and letting-go process is protracted. If this troubles you a lot, you may wish to seek out a professional and maybe someone who specializes in grief therapy. Much of what is proposed in this book can apply to a parent of a deceased young adult. Since the focus of the apology is on you as the parent, carrying out a ritual of writing out an apology and possibly visiting the grave of your young adult and reading it may be immensely helpful.

Many believe that we can somehow connect to our loved ones who have died with our thoughts, and if this is the case for you, then carrying out this ritual of writing and/or speaking to and apologizing to this loved one can be quite healing. But remember the apology is primarily about letting go of past shortcomings or failures as a parent. If you are struggling with the loss of a young person and feel a need to apologize through a process described above, take someone, a professional or close friend, with you on that journey.

CHAPTER 13

The "I'm Sorry" Impact

Sorry will change you.

Apology Changes You

You need to find the difference in your heart and in your actions and not in the impact on your young adult. The critical question is not: "Have they changed?" The critical question is: "Have I/we changed?" Although saying "I'm sorry" is a gift to your child, it also represents a gift you give yourself. It's important to note that saying you're sorry is designed to address our shortcomings as parents and let go of the emotions that have kept us bound in negative ways to our children. It's about changing our hearts and opening up space for loving these adult children without the interference of emotions and memories that cause us pain.

At the end of moving through a practice of apology, we as parents should feel differently toward our adult child. In *Do You Speak Millennial "ese"?* I introduced the concept of doing your own report card. Essentially this means looking in the mirror and asking how you are doing on these practices that parents need to strengthen. In this case, you can look into the mirror and ask the following questions, the answers to which do not depend on your young adult.

- Have I identified, in my review of my parenting or through my young adult's communications, actions that deserve an apology?

- Have I stepped up and taken responsibility for these actions that deserve an apology?

- Have I explicitly communicated my sincere regret and apology for these actions to my young adult without qualifications?

- Do I feel a relief or lessening of the burden of guilt or shame I have felt for these actions?

- Have my communication and how I engage my young adult changed with less defensiveness and reactivity?

We should find that we act differently after apologizing, since we won't have the interference of unaddressed issues and events of the past. When we have not said we are sorry, we are susceptible to defensiveness and reactivity that can color our words, body language, and tone. In the end, by failing to apologize we risk freeing both our young adult and ourselves from the past and also jeopardize our relationship in the future.

Apology May Not Change Them

There are several possible responses to an apology delivered to a young adult child.

- Your young adult acknowledges your apology.

- Your young adult may excuse you or say there is no need to apologize. In such case indicate you need to say you're sorry even though they may not believe there is a need.

- The young adult accepts the apology.

- The young adult accepts the apology and offers forgiveness.

- The young adult receives your apology but refuses to accept it.

- The young adult uses your disclosure of an offense you described to blackmail you. Since you did _____ you should now do _____.

- Your young adult uses your admission as a basis for excusing their behavior now or in the past.

- The young adult does not acknowledge your apology and refuses to communicate with you.

In the last instance, a relationship may be broken and nothing you do seems to make any difference. A broken home has been a phrase used to describe families where the parents have divorced. But I would broaden this definition to also cover broken homes where there has been a divorce between the siblings or the parents and their adult children. These divorces can be as painful if not more so than those between the parents. I see many such broken families in my private practice and it is heartbreaking to observe.

Sometimes there are mental health issues that complicate the letting-go process, and if a young person doesn't address these, they may not be capable of responding to a parent's apology. Parents of one young adult had made numerous efforts to reach out, apologize, and request contact but to no avail. This young adult and spouse are seeking counseling related to this estrangement but the parents have been severely limited in any communications. In such a case, a grieving is necessary for the loss of this closeness while continuing to communicate a receptivity to reconnecting when this couple feel able and willing.

Estrangement or alienation is sometimes used to describe the cutoff relationship between parents and their young adult children. It is painful and widespread. Joshua Coleman, who is cochair of the Council on Contemporary Families calls this breach in parent-young adult relations a "silent epidemic."[6] Way too many families have empty chairs at holidays and the absence of phone calls on birthdays and special occasions. Parents need to take the high road and say they are sorry, as they are able to identify their behavior that has played a role in this rift. But it may not be enough to heal the wounds. Sometimes it was something that was done or said that was viewed as offensive, insensitive, or rejecting by the young adult that they just can't get over. So what can you do?

First, start with recognition that your adult child may not want to have any association with you and there is nothing you can do about this. You cannot force or compel your adult child to connect with you. This will help you deal with the need to control or to believe that if you just say or do the "right" thing the relationship will be restored. Such a belief can lead to much pain and disappointment. So expect nothing but do what you can.

Second, try to find out the source of the rift between you and your adult child if you do not know this. In such cases, the first step is to ask for understanding of what has led to the distance and what can the parent do to close this gap. I'd recommend meeting at a restaurant or someplace outside of either your home or theirs to have a conversation about the estrangement and what you can do to address this. Be sure to take the high road, listen nonjudgmentally, and be receptive to what they say as to the cause of the rift. In the earlier practice book *Can You Speak Millennial "ese"?* I offer suggestions how to listen nonjudgmentally and ask appropriate open-ended questions. Determine to not be defensive, take notes to remember, and indicate that you would like to think about what they have said and then get back to them. If they are unwilling to meet, offer to communicate with email.

Third, once you have established the source of the rift, take responsibility for the incident without the "buts" or qualifications described above. Then follow the guidelines for an effective apology and construct a communication. Have a spouse and possibly an outside party read the communication as if they were your young adult receiving it and give you feedback on how you could say things more effectively. It's important to validate their perception of what happened even though your memory of it may be different. They have a right to their perception. Our role is to apologize for whatever we can that was part of contributing to that perception.

Fourth, if this fails to lead to reconciliation or a better relationship, you may offer to bring in a third party to help with understanding. In this regard, you could ask your clergy or close friend of the family or propose that you seek a therapist who might be able to help with communication and understanding.

Finally, you just may continue to be shut out of your young adult's life. This can be doubly painful if there are grandchildren involved. But no response or lack thereof should be an excuse to respond in kind by cutting them off. We love our kids no matter what, and we must continue to take the high road of reaching out in love. We may only be able to send cards and/or gifts at holidays and birthdays or infrequent texts or emails sharing something positive about our feelings and memories of them. Don't stop because "we" need to do this. We are wired to connect to our kids no matter what age or what may have separated us. Understand that your young adult is suffering as well since they are wired to love their parents.

CHAPTER 14

When Not to Apologize

First of all, don't apologize if you are not ready just because you should or to make yourself feel better. If you don't feel the remorse or regret and some level of empathy, your apology will likely come off as insincere. In such cases you may want to talk to your young adult and try to understand more what they experienced and why it hurt them. As stated earlier, you may want to reflect—put yourself in their shoes if possible and come up with two or three reasons why an apology is deserved.

Second, do you always have to apologize for communications, decisions, or acts with which your young adult disagrees? The short answer is "no!" Sometimes we have to make the tough call, set limits, establish constraints to ensure safety, and say no. In an upcoming book *No Is Not a Four-Letter Word,* I will address the practice of tough love. In this book, I will discuss actions such as setting limits, establishing boundaries, and indicating what you as a parent will and will not do.

In my own experience, I was seen as overprotective by my two daughters well into their twenties. When they were home and under my control, probably an illusion on my part, I restricted them from driving or going with friends to nightclubs in Minneapolis. We lived in a suburb of the Twin Cities and there were regular reports of incidents of violence in the entertainment district of Minneapolis. As a psychologist I was well aware of the statistic related to sexual abuse of girls up to the age of eighteen. Research conducted by the Centers for Disease Control (CDC) estimates that approximately one in four girls are sexually abused before the age of eighteen. I make no apologies for being overprotective.

Once when I found empty beer bottles stashed away outside of my son's room in the basement, my wife and I grounded him for a month. It seemed a bit harsh at the time but it enabled him to disconnect from some friends that were not the best influence. Later he indicated that he thought that he may not have become captain of the football team had we not cut off his connections with this partying group of friends at the time we did. It's rare but sometimes you get a thank you for something that at the time your child or teen thought was an overreaction.

Finally, be thoughtful about why you are apologizing and what the impact might be. You should not apologize just to get something off your chest. An apology should not be done simply to make a parent feel better. It should be thoughtful, sincere, and something that your child would likely see as an appropriate action on your part. In the AA tradition Step 8 involves "making a list of all persons we have harmed and be willing to make amends to them." But Step 9 reads "make direct amends to those people, whenever possible, except when to do so would injure them or others." So you can ask the question of whether this apology and possible effort to make amends would be helpful or potentially hurtful. For instance, if you had been abusive to your child and made efforts in the past to face this but your child then or now just wants to move on, you need to respect this and not dredge up the specifics of this offense just so you can feel better.

In conclusion, err on the side of apology. The upside of apologizing to our kids is greater than the downside and will help us be a better parent and a better person. It's not the only practice we need to undertake to help launch our kids but it is an important one for both their sakes and ours.

Be brave . . . be vulnerable . . . be first.

CHAPTER 15

Resources

Keepers

My friend Terry Paulson, who is a leadership consultant, motivational speaker, and humorist, likes to have people identify "keepers." These are key points, recommendations, and ideas that people can take with them and apply after hearing a lecture or reading a book like this. You may have identified and/or highlighted some keepers as you have read through this book. Trust your selection of what's important.

Here's my list of keepers or reminders that might prove helpful to you.

1. It is never too late to apologize to your young adult. Why wait?

2. As parents we all make mistakes. We are not alone. If a convention were to be held for perfect parents, no one would attend.

3. An apology consists of a sincere statement of regret (saying "I'm sorry") for a mistake or action that was experienced as harmful to your young adult.

4. Apologizing is not for wimps! It takes courage, strength, vulnerability, humility, and a willingness to be first.

5. Apology admits mistakes, says I care, models honesty and empathy, and contributes to a better you and a healing of the relationship.

6. Apologizing as a parent sets our young adult free. It says to them: it was my fault, not yours. It can melt away longstanding blame, hurt, and resentment the young adult may be harboring.

7. There is a right way to apologize—show regret or remorse, take responsibility, offer to repair, and promise change.

8. There is a wrong way to apologize—saying I'm sorry but or if; I'm sorry you feel; I'm sorry I didn't mean it—as well as blanket or partial apologies. Saying I did my best as a parent is not an apology; it's an excuse.

9. Sorry will change you as a parent by enabling you to let go of the past and how this binds you to the young adult. It is also the first step to forgiving yourself.

10. Sorry may not change your young adult, and an apology sought for this end is not sincere or effective. If nothing changes, never give up for your sake as well as your young adult's.

Call to Action

What are you willing to do in the next twenty-four hours? Check those you can start right away.

_____Come up with my own set of keepers from this book and commit to discussing them with my partner or good friend.

_____Sit down and think about my feelings of guilt or remorse and identify what I said or did that was harmful.

_____ Interview my young adult with the interview questions in chapter 10.

_____ Discuss with my spouse or good friend the contents of this book and my thoughts regarding my need to apologize.

_____ Read about apology in one or more of the suggested readings at the end of this book.

_____ Review the list of reasons why it's hard to apologize and discuss the barriers I have to my desire to apologize.

_____ Craft a letter of apology to my young adult.

_____ Deliver a letter of apology to my young adult.

_____ Put this book on a shelf for later consideration. If this is the choice, consider what might be holding you back from one or more of the actions above. Will you be brave? Will you be vulnerable? Will you be first?

Suggested Reading on Apology

Brown, Brené. *Daring Greatly: How the Courage to Be Vulnerable Transforms the Way We Live, Love, Parent, and Lead.* New York: Penguin Putnan, 2012.

Chapman, Gary and Jennifer Thomas. *When Sorry Isn't Enough: Making Things Right with Those You Love.* Chicago: Northfield Publishing, 2013.

Engel, Beverly. *The Power of Apology.* New York: John Wiley and Sons, 2001.

Kador, John. *Effective Apology.* San Francisco: Berrett-Koehler Publishers, 2009.

Lazare, Aaron. *On Apology.* New York: Oxford Univerity Press, 2004.

Learner, Harriet. *Why Won't You Apologize?* New York: Simon and Schuster, 2017.

1. Roy J. Lewicki, Beth Polin, and Robert B. Lount Jr., "An Exploration of the Structure of Effective Apologies," *Negotiation and Conflict Management Research,* 9, no. 2 (May 2016): 177–96. doi: 10.1111/ncmr.12073

2. Harriet Lerner, *Why Won't You Apologize? Healing Big Betrayals and Everyday Hurts* (New York: Touchstone, 2017).

3. Brené Brown, *I Thought It Was Just Me* (New York: Gotham Books, 2007) and *The Gifts of Imperfection* (Center City, MN: Hazelden, 2010).

4. Kelly Dickenson, "Total Regret," *Psychology Today* (May/June 2014).

5. Dennis Praeger, *Happiness Is a Serious Problem* (New York: Harper Collins, 1998).

6. See Joshua Coleman's website for specific help with the problem of estrangement http://www.drjoshuacoleman.com/

Made in the USA
Las Vegas, NV
11 January 2021

15729125R00036